W9-BXQ-425

WHY SO MANY

DENOMINATIONS?

REVELATION'S FOUR HORSEMEN
PROVIDE AN ANSWER

MARK FINLEY
with STEVEN MOSLEY

Pacific Press Publishing Association
Boise, Idaho
Oshawa, Ontario, Canada

Edited by B. Russell Holt
Designed by Tim Larson
Cover designed by Judi Morrison
Typeset in 10/12 Century Schoolbook

Unless otherwise noted, all Scripture quotations are taken from the New King James Version.
The authors assume responsibility for the accuracy of all facts and quotations cited in this book.

Library of Congress Cataloging-in-Publication Data:

Finley, Mark, 1945-
    Why so many denominations? Revelation's four horsemen provide an answer / Mark Finley with Steven Mosley.
        p.   cm.
    ISBN 0-8163-1218-4
    1. Seventh-day Adventists—Apologetic works. 2. Four Horsemen of the Apocalypse. 3. Adventists—Apologetic works. 4. Sabbatarians—Apologetic works. I. Mosley, Steven R., 1952- II. Title.
BX6154.F45   1994
286. 7'32—dc20   93-47907
                                                          CIP

94 95 96 97 98 • 5 4 3 2 1

Contents

Before You Turn This Page

Truth sure seems elusive these days! Some people spend a lifetime trying to find it—and come up empty. Others think they have found it, only to discover they are face to face with a counterfeit. They've accepted a fraud—and possibly a deadly fraud, at that. Remember Jonestown and Waco! The cults have a certain pull. Their authoritative answers strike a responsive chord in all of us. In contrast to many mainline churches whose teachings are so watered down you can believe about anything, the definiteness of the cults may seem attractive.

In their attempt to keep from being labeled either "narrow-minded fanatics" or "religious bigots," many thinking people have completely rejected the idea that God has a true church. Yet, deep within all of us, there is an inborn desire to really know. Does God have a movement on earth today? If so, how can I find it? Why are there so many denominations? Where did they originate?

Jesus' words are reassuring: "You shall know the truth, and the truth shall make you free" (John 8:32). And later, He adds, "Sanctify them by Your truth. Your word is truth" (John 17:17). God's Word reveals His truth, and millions have found it! These individuals have recaptured the essence of biblical, New Testament Christianity. You can be among them. You can discover the faith of Jesus and His disciples. You need not be deceived by a counterfeit.

In the truth-filled chapters of this book, you will find answers to your deepest questions. You will understand why there are so many different churches and find principles to distinguish truth from error. Revelation, the Bible's last book, pulsates with God's truth for today. Rather than being obscure, it is plain.

The book you hold in your hands can change your life. It takes a refreshing, straightforward, no-nonsense approach that deals candidly with the issues. It grapples with the struggle that has existed between truth and error through the centuries. It unmasks Satan's deceptive plot to counteract truth. Steven and I earnestly desire God's Holy Spirit to guide your mind as you read these pages. Without the guidance of the Holy Spirit, all attempts to discover truth are in vain.

With His guidance, however, discovering God's will is certain. May your mind be open to His guidance as you read.

Mark Finley

Testament Christianity. We really want to get back to the pure teachings of Jesus and the disciples."

That's the bottom line for most Christian fellowships. They want to be the kind of organization that reflects the church Jesus Himself founded. They want to build on the Solid Rock, the Chief Cornerstone, the Saviour and Lord, Jesus Christ.

The bloodstained sands of time speak of a New Testament faith worth dying for. Early Christians were willing to give their lives for the Lord Jesus. Phileas, executed for his faith in A.D. 306 at Alexandria, was one of these. But before he died, he left a beautiful testimony for his faith, recorded by eyewitnesses.

Phileas was young and wealthy, and he came from the upper class. He'd served honorably in public affairs and had a wife and children. For him, becoming a Christian involved risking everything, but he gladly took that risk.

After his arrest, the Roman prefect of Egypt tried to persuade him to give up his faith: "Free your mind of this madness that has seized on it," he urged Phileas.

Phileas calmly replied, "I have never been mad and am quite sane now."

"Very well, then," the prefect replied. "Sacrifice to the gods."

Phileas answered that he could sacrifice only to one God.

"What kind of sacrifices does your God like?" he was asked.

"Purity of heart, sincere faith, and truth."

During the whole ordeal of the interrogation, as Phileas stood before the judge with his weeping family in the courtroom, he testified eloquently for his faith.

When pressed again to give in, Phileas said, "The Saviour of all our souls is Jesus Christ, whom I serve in these chains. . . . I have given much thought to my situation, and I am determined to suffer for Christ."

Shortly afterward, Phileas was beheaded. People like him challenge us to be faithful to the purity of the gospel. Individuals like him call us back.

But Phileas was not alone. There were many others in the early church who gladly gave up their lives. The church historian Eusebius was an eyewitness of the suffering of believers in Egypt. He wrote:

> We saw the most marvelous inspiration, a force which was truly divine, and the readiness of those who had faith in the Christ of God.
>
> Immediately when sentence had been pronounced on one group, another party came before the tribunal . . . acknowledging themselves Christians and remaining unmoved before dangers and torments of all kinds. Indeed, they reasoned bravely and clearly concerning the service of God. . . . Lighthearted and happy, they received with joy the final sentence of death. They sang hymns and offered thanksgiving to the God of all until their last breath.

No wonder that, in the end, these people overwhelmed even the might of the Roman Empire! Their devotion to Jesus was greater than their fear of death.

This is the ideal that all denominations try to point back to—the purity and genuineness of New Testament religion. It may be difficult to believe, with some two hundred major denominations beckoning to us from the Yellow Pages, but almost every single Christian church is rooted in the same idea, the same longing to recapture something that has been lost. We want to experience in our lives that early intensity of faith.

Jesus—the center of the early church

With this in mind, may I suggest the first step we need to take in answering the question Why so many denominations? We need to look carefully at exactly what we're all trying to get back to. What are we trying to recapture? What was the New Testament church really like?

The New Testament reveals principles that guide us in our journey to find truth. It describes the essence of Christianity clearly. There is one important question that will simplify the entire process when we answer it. A question that best tells us what the New Testament church was like. And that question is simply: What does the New Testament *emphasize*? What does it keep coming back to, over and over, as most important?

I suggest we zero in on the epistles. After all, these are letters addressed specifically to individual churches; they are attempts to build up the church.

Can we summarize what we find in these letters?

Well, first of all, there's a pattern. Most of the epistles begin with a chapter or two celebrating Christ's glory. Paul waxes eloquent, describing Christ as the firstborn of all creation, the image of the invisible God, seated at the right hand of God in the heavenly realms (see Colossians 1:15; Ephesians 1:20). The epistles start by painting a vivid picture of what a wonderful Saviour and Lord and Friend Jesus is.

Then they progress to dealing with a wide variety of practical problems these churches faced. But the advice given can be summarized very simply: love one another; forgive each other; build up one another; accept one another just as God has accepted you in Christ. Those are the phrases repeated over and over.

So, can we figure out what the New Testament emphasizes? Yes, I think we can. It emphasizes devotion to

Christ and love for one another. You can't read the New Testament epistles without being impressed by those themes.

Paul, in fact, is very explicit about what he has come to see as the most important aspect of early Christianity. Listen to Philippians 3:8,

> I also count all things loss for the excellence of the knowledge of Christ Jesus my Lord, for whom I have suffered the loss of all things, and count them as rubbish, that I may gain Christ.

Devotion to Christ. That was the bottom line in Paul's life. And he combined with that a tireless love for other people.

This distinctive New Testament emphasis is also precisely what stands out in the history of the early church. It is the secret of its extraordinary power.

Do you know what was the first recorded response to the Christian movement? It was this: "How these Christians love one another!" That's what stood out; that's what people noticed. When Emperor Julian was trying to revive paganism, he blamed the rapid expansion of Christianity, in part, on what he called the Christians' "benevolence to strangers."

In a time when no one had heard of social services, Tertullian, an early church leader, wrote that funds were regularly collected "to feed the poor . . . for boys and girls who lack property and parents, and . . . for any who may be in the mines, on the penal islands, in prison . . . they become the pensioners of the confession."

The early church carried out those admonitions in the epistles in a wonderfully practical way.

And something else stood out as well: their joyful

devotion to Christ, even in times of fiercest persecution. The testimony of those who watched early believers die fills one with awe.

When a Roman governor told the young man Irenaeus, "Sacrifice to the emperor, or I will put you to the torture," Irenaeus replied, "I shall be happy if you do, for then I shall be able to share the sufferings of my Master."

When a beautiful young woman named Crispina was sentenced to be beheaded for refusing to offer incense to other gods, her only reply was, "Christo laudes ago [Christ be praised]."

When a former prostitute named Afra was arrested and ordered, "Get along to the capitol and sacrifice!" the woman replied, "My capitol is Christ, whom I keep before my eyes."

When a Roman proconsul told Bishop Polycarp that he would set him free if he would only curse Christ, the old Christian replied, "Eighty and six years have I served Him, and He did me no wrong. How can I blaspheme my King, who saved me?"

Devotion to Jesus Christ as Lord and Saviour. Love for one another. That is what the New Testament emphasizes. That is what stands out in the early church.

Why are churches so far apart?

This raises a question: If the Christian message is so simple, so basic, why are there so many denominations? If all Christians are trying to get back to the same thing, why do we end up so far apart?

Let me propose an answer: We Christians find ourselves far apart on many issues because some churches are emphasizing what the New Testament doesn't. They are complicating what the New Testament simplifies. They are splitting hairs and dissecting and debating and arguing over details, while the priceless message of love and faith in Christ gets left behind. In trying to get back to our roots, we are going on countless detours.

Let me give you some examples.

The New Testament has a great deal to say about how wonderful Christ is. The writers of Scripture concentrate on Christ Himself.

In the New Testament, Jesus is the Lord of glory, the One who is magnificent over all else. Today, some churches have moved away from the magnificent Christ to magnificent cathedrals. An elaborate liturgy has taken the place of the simplicity of gospel preaching. The traditions of the church have taken the place of the pure teachings of the Bible. Denominations have been wrangling over the right way to worship for centuries. Liturgy has, on occasion, actually become a battleground.

During the reign of Czar Alexis, the Russian church stood on the edge of revival and reformation. Groups of missionaries traveled through the land calling clergy and laypeople to sincere spiritual devotion. But then, tragically, the movement broke up.

Why?

Because they started disputing over correct forms of worship. The official church insisted that the sign of the cross be made with three fingers raised instead of two. They decreed that the threefold Alleluia, not the twofold, be sung in worship. Thousands of people, called "old ritualists," believed that such liturgical changes signaled the end of their religious faith. Many sacrificed their lives in opposition.

Why so many denominations? Because we spend so much time emphasizing what the New Testament doesn't. The apostles urge us eloquently to worship Christ. And we argue about forms and rituals, instead of simply worshiping Him from overflowing hearts.

Another example. When Christ presided over His Last Supper and instituted what has become known in most churches as the Communion service, He repeated these simple words, "Do this in remembrance of Me" (Luke 22:19). He wanted His followers, in taking the bread as His broken body and the drink as His shed blood, to remember His sacrifice on the cross.

That's it. "Remember, appreciate, be thankful. I'm doing all this for you, for your salvation."

In contrast to the simplicity of Jesus' words, various church groups have constructed elaborate doctrines around this sacrament. They've gone to great pains to create theologies of the bread and wine. And, incredibly enough, people who call themselves Christians have even been willing to torture and burn other believers for having a different perspective on this issue!

Listen to one remarkable interrogation. It comes to us from an ecclesiastical courtroom in sixteenth-century London. Bishop Bonner is quizzing a young man named Thomas Haukes, who stands condemned as a heretic.

"Do you not believe," the bishop asked indignantly, "that there remaineth in the blessed sacrament of the altar . . . the very body and blood of Christ?"

Haukes answered simply, "I do believe as Christ hath taught me."

This didn't satisfy Bishop Bonner. He wanted to know exactly what his prisoner thought Christ meant by the words, "Take, eat; this is My body" (Mark 14:22).

Haukes admitted he didn't agree with the current church doctrine, called *transubstantiation*, that the bread and wine actually became the literal body and blood of Jesus. He pointed out that none of the apostles had ever taught it.

This further angered the bishop. "Ah, sir! You will

have no more than the Scripture teacheth?"

That was precisely Thomas Haukes's position. He wanted to be taught from the Word of God. Earlier, this young man had been taunted for having "nothing but your little pretty God's book."

Haukes replied, "And is not that sufficient for my salvation?"

Bonner shot back, "Yes, it is sufficient for our salvation, but not for our instruction."

Thomas Haukes was burned at the stake.

Why?

Because he didn't believe we need something more "for our instruction" than what is clearly taught in Scripture, something more than what the New Testament emphasizes.

Why are there so many denominations? Because we emphasize what the New Testament doesn't. In trying to get back to our roots, we've gone on so many detours.

The doctrines of men

Listen to the clear teachings of Jesus. Speaking to the religious leaders of His day, and to those in all ages, He said: "In vain they worship Me, teaching as doctrines the commandments of men" (Mark 7:7).

Here you have it. The commandments of men—the traditions of the churches—have subtly replaced the teachings of Jesus.

All of us who want to recapture the purity and the power of the early church need to listen to this admonition from the apostle Paul: "I am afraid, lest as the serpent deceived Eve by his craftiness, your minds should be led astray from the simplicity and purity of devotion to Christ" (2 Corinthians 11:3, NASB).

"The purity and simplicity of devotion to Christ." That says it all, doesn't it? The Christian religion swept over the world because it centered around the person of Christ. It was allegiance to this Person, not just to an ideology or a set of doctrines, that turned the world upside down.

So if we're looking to get back to our roots in the early church, then we need to focus on these powerful themes: (1) devotion to Jesus Christ as Saviour and Lord and (2) love for one another. We need to emphasize what the New Testament emphasizes; we need to celebrate what the New Testament celebrates.

One of the clearest descriptions of the New Testament church in the Bible is found in Acts 2:41, 42:

> Those who gladly received his word were baptized; and that day about three thousand souls were added to them. And they continued steadfastly in the apostles' doctrine and fellowship, in the breaking of bread, and in prayers.

Nothing extraordinary in these words—just a group of people totally dedicated to Christ, gladly accepting His Word, following His teachings, seeking God in prayer, and fellowshiping in love with one another. But these worshipers turned the world upside down.

Jesus only

In this book, we'll be exploring ways in which our churches can be more healthy and more genuinely reflective of that spiritual power of the New Testament church. We'll be looking at other reasons why there are so many denominations. But what we've covered in this chapter is the foundation of everything that comes afterward. If we don't get back to Christ Himself, we're going in the wrong direction; we're off on a detour.

Implicit in many of our denominational beliefs is this

hidden assumption: We need more than just Jesus. He's not enough. We have to have Jesus *plus* a certain body of tradition. We have to elaborate in areas where He didn't speak. We have to fill out the gaps in New Testament teaching.

Friends, it's not true that we need more than just Jesus. We need more *of* just Jesus—not more *than* just Jesus. We need pure devotion to Christ; we need His love in our hearts.

Would you join with me in a prayer for all believers in Christ around the world? In our hearts, we all want to get back to the right place, the place at Jesus' feet. We want to bring His Spirit into our congregations and have His life fill our churches. Let's begin that journey right now on our knees.

* * * * *

Father mine, I want to praise You for the priceless gift of Your Son, Jesus Christ, who gave Himself up for the sins of the world. He is Lord over all, filling all things everywhere, the true Head of Your church. We want to dedicate ourselves to Him right now in a special way. Make us truly members of Christ's body. Instill in us a devotion that nothing can diminish, nothing can sweep away. Keep the living Christ before our eyes always. In His name I ask. Amen.

Can the Church Fail?

They came galloping all unexpectedly out of the sky toward an imprisoned writer named John—the four horsemen of the Apocalypse. It was surely one of his more startling visions. The horsemen appeared to be omens of some great cataclysm. But what must have shocked John even more was that these riders of Revelation symbolized what would happen to Christ's own beloved church!

Most Christians are familiar with Jesus' great intercessory prayer recorded in John 17. Speaking of His followers, He said, "I . . . pray . . . that they all may be one" (verses 20, 21). Well, that unity of faith hasn't happened, has it? The one body of Christ has broken up into hundreds of factions.

Why? Why so many denominations?

We have already discovered that one of the main reasons. Christians have emphasized what the New Testament doesn't. The Biblical emphasis on love and loyalty to Christ has been replaced by a host of church traditions. At times, well-meaning religious teachers have substituted their own ideas for the teachings of Christ.

Let's discover the second main reason. It has to do with the nature of institutions—with what happens to organizations.

We will start by looking carefully at what the church Jesus established was like. We get a good picture from an incident in the life of Paul.

The apostle was being attacked by a mob outside the temple in Jerusalem. These people believed that Paul had defiled their holy place by bringing a Greek friend inside. They seemed intent on tearing him to pieces as a demonstration of their religious indignation.

Fortunately, the Roman commander in Jerusalem heard about the commotion and hurried to the scene with his soldiers. As the Romans approached, the mob pulled back from the man they were about to beat to death.

The commander then proceeded to arrest Paul. Lying there in his own blood, he was bound with two chains. When Paul asked what crime he'd committed, the mob began yelling out all kinds of accusations. The noise grew so ferocious that the Roman commander thought he'd better get Paul into a nearby barracks.

The Roman soldiers barely managed to shove their way through the mob with the prisoner, but finally they reached the steps of the barracks and relative safety. However, before they could go in, Paul revived himself enough to make a request. He wanted to speak to the crowd.

That strikes me as quite remarkable. This man had narrowly escaped a brutal death and was just about to be taken to a place of safety, but now he wanted to turn toward those contorted faces and have a few words!

For some reason, the commander consented. Paul stood up on the steps and motioned to the crowd. When they quieted a bit, he said, "Men, brethren, and fathers, hear my defense" (Acts 22:1). He then proceeded to tell the story of his conversion, and through it, he made an eloquent appeal to his countrymen.

Paul always made an appeal whenever he had an opportunity, and his appeal was always the same: "Repent, believe in Jesus Christ, and be saved." He was always extending to men and women the pardon and grace that Christ had offered from the cross. He had extended it to philosophers in Athens, to idol worshipers in Antioch, and now to his would-be murderers in Jerusalem.

Two views of salvation

To me, that is the church of the book of Acts in a nutshell—always sharing the good news, no matter what; fearlessly proclaiming the revolutionary message of salvation in Christ. This message comes through loud and clear in the New Testament: There is a sure way into the kingdom, and that way is Jesus Christ.

The apostle John writes to all who believe in the name of the Son of God, so that, he says, "you may *know* that you have eternal life" (1 John 5:13, emphasis supplied).

The apostle Peter, in his first epistle, assures his readers that by believing in Christ they are receiving the outcome of their faith, the salvation of their souls (see 1 Peter 1:9).

And of course, Paul himself, through all his letters, never tires of proclaiming that salvation comes by grace through faith in Christ.

The New Testament church had a clear, forceful message. Those early Christians said, "This is where we stand—in the grace of Christ. Come stand with us, and you will experience eternal life." That message swept over the world and transformed it.

Now let's fly forward several centuries and take another look at the Christian church. If we stopped in the thirteenth century, this is what we'd find. A rich man on his deathbed, feverishly writing a will. What's his major concern? Making sure payment is made to the local cathedral so that masses will be said for his soul after he dies. Why? Because he hopes that will shorten his time in purgatory.

We would find men and women out on the roads of Europe, walking on long pilgrimages to places like Canterbury or Rome. Why? Because a priest ordered them to do it as a penance for their sins. Someone who had committed a serious offense might be obliged to fast on certain days of the week for the rest of his life.

In the Middle Ages, we would sometimes find individuals undertaking penances for others in return for payment. One wealthy man got through a seven-year fasting penance in three days because he hired 840 followers to fast with him! Such practices later developed into the sale of indulgences. Christians imagined they could buy into the surplus merit that the saints had accumulated in order to cover their own sins.

The church that had once proclaimed the grace of Christ so freely and powerfully was now intent on the promotion of holy relics and the merit of saints, shrines, and ceremonies. It's hard to conceive of two more different views of salvation.

The New Testament believer rejoiced in Christ's gracious acceptance. The medieval believer prayed that he wouldn't die before his penance was complete, hoping against hope that he would somehow find a place in heaven.

A pure and victorious church

The state of Christendom in the Middle Ages raises some very perplexing questions: Wasn't this the same church that Jesus Himself had founded? Didn't He promise that the gates of hell would not prevail against it? What happened? How did the Bible-based, Christ-centered, Spirit-filled church of God sink so low?

I think that a vivid scene from the book of Revelation gives us an answer. It's found in the first part of chapter 6. There the Lamb, or Christ, is pictured opening a series of seals. He is, in effect, unrolling the scrolls of history, giving John the Revelator views of the future.

This is what John says in verse 2:

> I looked, and behold, a white horse. And he who sat on it had a bow; and a crown was given to him, and he went out conquering and to conquer.

White is the symbol of apostolic purity, and Jesus, who wears a crown, is the One riding that horse. He goes out "conquering and to conquer."

When a Roman general conquered an opponent, he triumphantly returned on a white horse, leading the victor's parade. White is a symbol of both apostolic purity and of conquest or victory. In the first century, the apostolic church powerfully conquered evil. It swept over the world, conquering with the gospel. The white-horse period represents the Christian church going forth with power.

The decline of the church

But then John sees the scene change. Satan fiercely opposes the church. Another horse, of fiery red, emerges. Associated with this horse are a great sword and people killing one another.

This horse represents the period of persecution. The church turned red with the blood of martyrs. Countless believers lost their lives to wild beasts in the Colosseum. They were mercilessly hunted down in North Africa and even tracked down in Europe. The time of persecution lasted from about A.D. 100 to A.D. 323.

Next, John sees a black horse in his vision. Its rider holds a pair of scales in his hands. What could this represent?

Well, persecution ended for good when Christianity became the official religion of the Roman Empire. Pagans by the thousands decided to join the church. Unfortunately, they brought with them many pagan practices. And even more tragically, the church all too often accommodated these practices.

One pagan practice that crept into the church was the worship of images. Church officials reinterpreted, or simply deleted, the commandment forbidding idols and images. Some pagan idols were given new names and brought into churches. An image dedicated to Jupiter became a statue of Peter. A fertility figure became Mary, mother of Jesus.

Another example is the change of the Bible Sabbath. God established the Sabbath as a sign of His creative authority in Genesis. He emphasized it in the Ten Commandments, written on tables of stone with His own finger, when He emphatically declared, "Remember the Sabbath day, to keep it holy" (Exodus 20:8).

Jesus left a positive example of Sabbath keeping by attending church each Sabbath. His disciples kept the Bible Sabbath decades after His crucifixion (see Luke 4:16; Acts 17:1-3; 18:1-4).

Listen to an incredible prediction by the prophet Daniel regarding a time when church and state would unite to change God's law. Speaking of a power that would "speak pompous words against the Most High" and that would "persecute the saints of the Most High," Daniel says this power would also "intend to change times and law" (Daniel 7:25).

Sun worship was very popular throughout the Roman Empire. To accommodate the pagans, church and state united to firmly establish Sunday as the day of worship. Sunday worship disassociated Christianity from the Jews on the one hand and made baptized pagans feel more comfortable on the other. There is a problem, however: the change was contrary to God's divine command, "Remember the Sabbath day, to keep it holy" (Exodus 20:8).

The black-horse period of the church was truly an age of compromise—a period when truth was weighed in the balances and found wanting. It symbolizes the darkness that settled over the church as the light of the gospel was extinguished by pagan superstition.

A spiritually dead church

Finally, John sees a fourth horse galloping toward him. It is very pale, and its rider is named Death; Hades follows close behind. What has happened? Something almost inconceivable: the church has died spiritually; it is no longer what it once was.

Yes, the church that Christ established, once white with apostolic purity and a conquering force in the world, has been reduced to a ghostly horse ridden by death, fleeing Hades.

These four horsemen of the Apocalypse are a graphic depiction of the history of the church. God knew what would happen. God knew about the almost unthinkable tragedy that would befall His church.

So, you see, these pictures in the book of Revelation, written down in the time of John, were both a prediction and an anguished warning: "This is what can happen to the church! Yes, it's a conquering force now, but it can lose its purity and power; it can die!"

It also points up a truth that we all must face: God will not compel any church group to obey Him, any more than He will force an individual to obey Him. He doesn't rule His church with an iron hand. He leads it with a gentle touch.

Why are there so many denominations? Because institutions decay. Churches fail to be faithful to their sacred trust. They run out of steam. Their spiritual life drains away. Their commitment is diluted. Our ultimate faith cannot be in any organization, no matter how noble it may appear. That's what the four horsemen of the Apocalypse are telling us.

Well, you may be wondering, what hope is there, then? How can we have certainty in this world? If even a church that Christ founded can die, how can we be sure of a place to stand today? How can we have a message to believe in?

Let me suggest an answer by taking you to one of the most remarkable scenes in history. A former monk has been called to account for his beliefs before an imperial assembly. Charles himself, the holy Roman emperor, sits in pomp and splendor. Around him are representatives of papal power in their imposing robes. And facing them is the former monk, the son of a tin miner, one man very much alone, without a shred of authority. But he does cling to one thing: A growing faith in the sufficiency of God's Word. His name is Martin Luther.

He stands before that imperial assembly and declares, "Universal complaints testify that by the laws of the popes the consciences of men are racked."

The emperor shouts indignantly, "No!"

Luther calmly responds, "Why may not a worm like me ask to be convicted of error from the prophets and the Gospels? If I am shown my error, I will be the first to throw my books into the fire."

An archbishop present tells him he has no right to call into question "the most holy orthodox faith," confirmed by "sacred councils" and "so many famous men."

He then demands of Luther, "Do you or do you not repudiate your . . . errors?"

Luther has to make a choice. He has to choose between what appears to be certain death and what he sees as the clear teaching of Scripture. He chooses the latter, saying, "Unless I am convicted by Scripture and plain reason—I do not accept the authority of popes and councils—my conscience is captive to the Word of God. . . . Here I stand, I cannot do otherwise."

What stand was Martin Luther taking? He had raised Paul's proclamation of justification by faith as a weapon against the whole system of relics and penances and indulgences. The New Testament made salvation so clear and simple; why was the church making it so complicated?

Rescued by the Word of God

Why was Luther standing alone? That's a good question. Many today don't realize that there were others in his day who desired to reform the church. Many others wanted to curb the corruption and superstition. They hadn't been able to move the church.

But Martin had found a place to stand; that made all the difference. He was standing on the Word of God. Against the enormous power of the medieval church, he raised a protest. And incredibly enough, with the Word of God alone in his hands, he found that he had tremendous leverage. The Christian world toppled over into reformation.

Friends, only the Word of God can reform the church. That's how it has always been. Think of God's church in the Old Testament. How often did the Israelites sink into apostasy? What saved them from the brink of extinction? They were saved by someone coming in and fearlessly proclaiming, "Thus sayeth the Lord." Yes, the prophets proclaiming the Word of God rescued the church.

What was the church like in Jesus' day? The traditions of the Pharisees and Sadducees had all but strangled the life out of it. The church was a pale horse ridden by Death. How was it rescued? It was rescued by Jesus, saying, "It is written."

Institutions decay. Churches fail. The only thing that can rescue us is the Word of God. That's the only place where we can stand.

The Word of God challenges the church, reforms the church. That's why religious traditions must always be held accountable to Scripture. The church can never stand over the Word; the Word of God must always stand over the church.

In his first epistle, Peter quotes these words from Isaiah: "All flesh is as grass, and all the glory of man as the flower of the grass. The grass withers, and its flower falls away, but the word of the Lord endures forever" (1 Peter 1:24, 25).

Everything fades, everything decays, *except* the Word of God. It is, as the apostles tell us, the royal law of liberty, the firm foundation, profitable for correction and instruction. It is, according to Hebrews, a living and powerful sword that pierces our innermost being.

All through history, even when the church has failed most tragically, the Word of God has endured. Even when the institutions of Christianity have died spiritually, the Word has always been there to resuscitate, to bring back to life.

There have always been individuals, and groups of believers, who demonstrated loyalty to the Word of God. That's why there has always been a church that the gates of hell cannot prevail against. Sometimes it's an all-but-invisible church, but it has survived.

Take the early thirteenth century, for example. By that time, the established church had become rich and powerful. But then, a young man named Francis heard a few words from the Gospel of Matthew and proceeded to start a spiritual revolution. The words he heard were Christ's words to His disciples when He sent them out to preach and heal, carrying neither gold nor silver, neither bag nor staff (see Matthew 10:5-15).

Francis of Assisi took a stand on these few verses from the Word of God. Abandoning all worldly possessions, he began a ministry of preaching and caring for the poor and sick. His example of simplicity and service shook many awake in the medieval church.

In the fourteenth century, John Wycliffe took a stand amidst a very complacent church in England. He called his contemporaries back to the simplicity and purity of the New Testament faith. He and his followers worked against fierce opposition to make the Word of God available in the common language of the people.

John Huss also wielded the Word of God to great effect in the fourteenth century. He worked to reform the church in Bohemia. He emphasized the importance of personal piety in a time when religion seemed to consist entirely of ceremony. Huss also stressed the authority of Scripture and taught that only God can forgive sin.

A time of decision

These men and many others took courageous stands in a time of almost universal ignorance and superstition. They proclaimed ideas that were far ahead of their time. Why? Because they were standing on the Word of God.

They weren't content to just stand on church tradition; they weren't content simply to believe what the majority believed. They accepted the Scriptures as a reforming force in the life of the church. And the movements they founded carried forward God's truth in the world.

At some point, all of us have to make a very important decision. We have to decide where we're going to make our stand. Everyone, even the most secular person, accepts some kind of ultimate truth in his or her life. What will your truth be based on? Tradition, or the Word of God? The religion of the day, or the religion of the New Testament? That's the decision that will confront all of us. Do you know why? Because all institutions decay. Spiritual life slips away. God's truth gets watered down. Churches fail; they need to be reformed. And at some point, we'll have to make a decision: Do we go forward with God's Word, or do we simply hang on to tradition?

Tradition, of course, can be very comforting. We grow accustomed to a certain way of doing things; we grow accustomed to a certain system of beliefs. It can be very painful to break with custom and tradition.

But when the clear teachings of Scripture call us, we had better answer. When the Word of God comes into church and upsets the furniture, we had better be ready to clean house. We must be prepared to stand on the Word of God, even when it's uncomfortable, even when it upsets our religious routine.

Please remember, there's only one place of safety. Institutions come and go, but the Word of God remains forever. Churches rise and fall; the white horse of apostolic purity turns into the pale horse of death. But the Word of God remains a vital, living force for reform in our world.

Will you make a commitment with me right now? Will you decide to follow God's Word, wherever it may lead?

Will you choose to take a stand on the clear teachings of Scripture, no matter how inconvenient or uncomfortable that may be?

Yes, let's affirm the sovereignty of God's Word in our lives right now, as we pray.

* * * * *

Father in Heaven, thank You for being so patient with us. Thank You for being willing to work with human institutions. You've labored to win us over to the truth of Scripture; You've worked to reform the church down through the centuries. Today, Lord, we want to stand on the side of Jesus, not on the side of tradition. We commit our minds and hearts to the truths that You make plain to us in the Bible. Carry us forward in Your Word from this day on. In the name of our Saviour, Jesus Christ, I pray. Amen.

When Truth Marches On—and We Don't

There is an amusing, yet disturbing, story told regarding the racial prejudice that once existed in certain parts of America. An old black grandfather is discussing with his grandchildren a time when he was excluded from membership in a certain church.

"Well, let me tell you children about the time I tried to join that proper, rich-folks church up the road. I talked to the pastor, you see, and he tried to put me off—all kinds of excuses.

"I could see what was going on, so I told him, 'Pastor, I think I'll sleep on it. Maybe the Lord'll tell me what to do.'

"Well, next day the minister asks me, nervouslike, 'Did the Lord send you a message?'

" 'Yes, sir, He did,' I said. 'He told me it was no use. He said, "I've been trying to get in that same church Myself for ten years, and I still can't make it!" ' "

His grandchildren burst out laughing, but the seriousness in their eyes and their faces indicated they got the point.

It *is* sad, isn't it, when churches become identified by what they *exclude*? When all the focus is on keeping unwanted elements out, pretty soon you find there isn't that much left inside.

And this isn't just a problem of prejudice against certain races or classes. It applies to ideas as well—to truth. Sometimes we believers, in our efforts to hold on tightly to the truth, to keep it from being contaminated, find that it slips through our fingers.

You've probably heard it said of some very stubborn person: "It would take major surgery to get a new idea into his head." Unfortunately, that's sometimes true of churches. We can get to the point where all our windows are boarded up to keep error out, but very little light gets in.

We've been exploring the question Why so many denominations? We've seen that often church groups emphasize what the New Testament doesn't. We've seen that all institutions have a tendency to decay. In this chapter, we're going to look at the problem of getting stuck in a rut. What happens when the truth marches on—and we don't?

The pillar and ground of the truth

Let's start by getting a good look at what the church is *supposed* to be like. Paul gives us a picture in his first letter to a young pastor named Timothy. He calls the church "the house of God" and describes it this way: "The church of the living God, the pillar and ground of the truth" (1 Timothy 3:15).

It's pretty clear that one of the vital functions of the church is to serve as the guardian of God's truth.

There's a theme in the New Testament that many religious people don't understand very well. It's the theme of "progressive truth," or "progressive knowledge."

Listen to Paul, for example. He prays for the Colossians "that you may be filled with the knowledge of His will in all wisdom and spiritual understanding; that you may have a walk worthy of the Lord . . . increasing in the knowledge of God" (Colossians 1:9, 10).

Paul prays that believers will be increasing in knowledge, growing in their understanding of truth. He talks about putting on the new man "who is renewed in knowledge" (Colossians 3:10). He prays that the love of the Philippians "may abound still more and more in knowledge and all discernment" (Philippians 1:9).

The apostle Peter expands on the same theme. He urges believers to "grow in the grace and knowledge of our Lord and Saviour Jesus Christ" (2 Peter 3:18). He also says, "Add to your faith virtue, to virtue knowledge" (2 Peter 1:5).

How does the church serve as a pillar of the truth? By expanding it. By growing in knowledge. That's what believers are urged to do throughout the New Testament. If we stand still, the truth slips through our fingers. We can hold on to the truth only by reaching out for more.

Let me give you an example of a believer who did just that, someone who was wonderfully teachable—Dwight L. Moody. Mr. Moody, one of the most prolific evangelists of modern times, always had an eagerness to learn, to progress, to grow.

During one long preaching tour, Moody was traveling by train with a singer named Towner. A drunk with a badly bruised eye recognized Moody and started bawling out hymns. The evangelist didn't want to deal with the man and said, "Let's get out of here." But Towner told him that all the other cars were full.

Then a conductor came down the aisle. Moody, still irritated, stopped him and pointed out the drunk. The conductor went over and gently quieted the man. He bathed and bandaged his eye, then led him back to a seat where he could fall asleep.

After reflecting on this for a while, Moody told his

companion, "This has been a terrible rebuke to me." The conductor had acted like the good Samaritan, Moody said, while he himself had responded like an indifferent Pharisee. During the rest of that preaching tour, Moody told this story against himself in his messages.

Although Moody was a powerful preacher, he regularly sat at the feet of guest speakers with his Bible open—taking notes. Dwight Moody is an outstanding example of teachableness—one who was willing to learn, to grow, to discover more and more of God's truth.

The remnant

I believe a healthy church can be defined as "a movement of God's truth." Do you know that all through history, even in the darkest ages, there have been people who remained open to God's truths, who insisted on growing in the knowledge of Jesus Christ—instead of locking it up inside tradition?

We see this in the scriptural idea of "the remnant." When Israel and Judah went into captivity, it seemed that all God's people had succumbed to idolatry. But there was a faithful remnant, a group who came back with Ezra and Nehemiah to rebuild the temple in Jerusalem. As Haggai tells us: "All the remnant of the people, obeyed the voice of the Lord their God" (Haggai 1:12).

In New Testament times, most Jews rejected Jesus as the Messiah; they remained enclosed within their traditions. But not all. In Romans 11, Paul says of the Jews, "At this present time there is a remnant according to the election of grace" (verse 5).

God has always had a remnant—people who remained faithful by responding to His call, people who held on to the truth and reached out for more.

God has always had a remnant, even in the darkest ages. Take John Wycliffe and his followers in the fourteenth century, for example. Wycliffe reached past the ignorance and superstition of most of his fellow priests and took hold of the Bible, and the Bible alone, as the standard of truth. He took a courageous step out of the Dark Ages.

John Huss took another step in the fourteenth century. He reached past the bigotry and intolerance of his age to affirm that the individual owed ultimate loyalty only to the Word of God, not to human traditions.

Martin Luther took several more brave steps forward. He reached out and embraced the truth of justification by faith in a time when penances and indulgences had all but stamped it out. He proclaimed salvation by grace alone, by faith alone.

Later, the Anabaptist movement highlighted other truths: devotion to Christ, baptism of believers by immersion, and freedom of conscience.

In the eighteenth century, John Wesley reached past the dead formalism of the church of his day and rediscovered the truth of personal holiness, the life of discipleship. The church moved forward once again.

God has always had a remnant—people who held on to the truth by reaching out for more. And we are the beneficiaries of what they discovered. You and I today are standing on the shoulders of believers who reached out when it was dangerous to do so. Often we take for granted truths that cost blood, sweat, and tears.

A failure to grow

One of Ralph Waldo Emerson's farmer neighbors was looking over his library one day, and Emerson offered to lend him a book by Plato. The man had never heard of "this Plato fellow," but he took the book.

When he returned it, Emerson asked, "Did you enjoy the book?"

"I did that," the neighbor replied. "This Plato has a lot of my ideas."

Most of us are not aware of how indebted we are to those who've gone before—especially when it comes to Bible truth. But here's where we run into problems; here's a big reason why there are so many denominations. Instead of imitating the heroes of the faith in their *spirit* of discovery, we camp out around their discoveries and turn them into a doctrinal fortress.

Some have camped out around John Huss or Martin Luther. Some have camped out by John Calvin; others, by John Wesley. Now all of these men made wonderful discoveries in God's Word. But they didn't discover *everything*. Luther was willing to use the power of the state to impose his kind of religion. Calvin could be almost as intolerant as his state church enemies.

But guess what? After you've camped out, after you've made a fortress out of your doctrinal position, it's hard to move on. It's hard to pull up roots. When God's truth marches on, a lot of people get left behind. They are so intent on preserving the limited amount of truth they have, they fail to see the larger body of truth God desires them to have.

Friends, God's church is to be the pillar and support of the truth. It exists to help people *grow* in the grace and knowledge of the Lord Jesus Christ. Too many churches today are simply marking the spot of a great discovery in the past. They're not continuing to grow in the present. They end up identifying themselves by what they exclude.

Let me give you an example of the remarkable power of discovery. Helen Keller grew up in her own world, shut in by blindness and deafness. She became an almost uncontrollable "wild child" of intense passions.

One day while Helen was playing with a new doll,

her long-suffering tutor, Anne Sullivan, placed the toy in her lap and signed the letters *d-o-l-l* in Helen's palm repeatedly. But Helen didn't understand. As the tutor tried to connect this thing in her lap with the signs on her palm, the girl became agitated. She slammed the doll on the floor, breaking it in pieces.

Later, Miss Sullivan took the unruly girl down the path to the wellhouse. Someone was pumping water. Placing Helen's hand under the cool flow, the tutor spelled out *w-a-t-e-r* on her other palm. Suddenly, it clicked in the girl's mind.

Later, Helen recalled, "The mystery of language was revealed to me. I knew then that water meant the wonderful, cool something that was flowing over my hand. That living word awakened my soul; gave it light, hope, joy; set it free!"

Now Helen felt eager to learn. As they returned to the house, she began touching objects. Each one seemed to quiver with life. And then her fingers touched the broken doll. "My eyes filled with tears," she wrote, "for I realized what I had done, and for the first time I felt repentance and sorrow. That eve for the first time I longed for a new day to come."

The soul of this wild child, shut away in her own dark world, was awakened by the discovery of the living word. Friends, have you found a place where you can be awakened by the living Word of God? Are you willing to open your mind to new truths from God's Word? Are you willing to follow God's truth, laying aside man-made traditions?

God's last-day remnant

Remember that God has always had His remnant; there have always been believers who held on to the truth by reaching out for more. I believe there are such men and women today.

One of the glimpses that Revelation gives us of the future is found in chapter 12:17. We find there that the dragon (symbolizing Satan) was angry with the woman (or God's church) and went to make war with the remnant of her offspring. So, God will have His remnant to the very end.

Revelation continues to give us suggestions of what that remnant church will be like. Here are a few clues.

In Revelation 14, we see pictured God's final proclamation to the world. An angel flies from the midst of heaven with "the everlasting gospel to preach to those who dwell on the earth—to every nation, tribe, tongue, and people" (verse 6). This is the great commission given to the church; Christ's church is to reach every person with the gospel of Jesus Christ. So the work of the church is pictured here. Christ's true church will be a missionary evangelistic church.

Now listen to what this angel proclaims in a loud voice: "Fear God and give glory to Him, for the hour of His judgment has come; and worship Him who made heaven and earth, the sea and springs of water" (verse 7). There is a sense of urgency here. The angel calls humanity to offer worship to God because the hour of His judgment has come. Here is a message for the last days. Christ's church, His remnant, will emphasize His soon return.

I believe this is one of the characteristics of the remnant church today. It doesn't just offer worship as a nice option; it doesn't just proclaim a God who can help us through the day. It proclaims the urgency of giving God our unconditional allegiance because we are all subject to His authority, His judgment. He is coming soon!

Now, let's look at another clue. We just mentioned a verse in Revelation that speaks of Satan making war against the woman and the *remnant* of her seed. The last part of that verse, Revelation 12:17, actually describes the remnant. Here's what it says about the rest (or remnant) of her offspring: "who keep the commandments of God and have the testimony of Jesus Christ." The true church of God, the remnant, will keep His commandments. God's commandments are not out of date. They are eternal, unchanging principles of His government. They clearly reveal heaven's eternal standards of right. They were certainly not given for the Jews only. Jesus Himself said, "If you love Me, keep My commandments" (John 14:15).

God's laws don't become irrelevant; they need to be rediscovered. The spirit of discovery that animates the remnant people leads them to a deepening appreciation of God's principles and to a desire to apply them to more and more of life.

The remnant not only keep God's commandments, they have the testimony of Jesus Christ. Their faith is based on Jesus Christ—His life and death and resurrection.

So, here we have a thumbnail sketch of God's true church in the last days. It proclaims the everlasting gospel in the setting of God's judgment. It strives to keep all God's commandments. And it is guided by the testimony of Jesus.

Is there such a movement today? Well, it should be obvious that there are plenty of earnest, growing believers in almost all denominations. Churches arguing over which is the one true church of God don't paint a very pretty picture.

Following truth wherever it leads

After the apostasy of the Dark Ages, the Holy Spirit began gradually revealing the light of truth to His faithful followers. Truths long lost sight of through the ages were rediscovered—eternal truths such as the authority of the Scriptures, salvation through Christ alone, the second coming of Jesus, obedience to His law, the Sabbath, baptism by immersion, the real truth about life after death, etc.

Christianity had grown quite complacent at the time. The spirit of discovery had been lost. But the realization that Jesus Christ would soon invade human history awakened countless people from their slumber. Baptists and Methodists, Catholics and Episcopalians, as well as many unbelievers, were transformed by a new hope. They began studying the Bible as if it were a brand-new book, and they began making exciting discoveries about the scope of God's truth. These discoveries encompassed everything, from Creation to Revelation, from healthful living to the state of the dead, from Sabbath rest to the work of the Holy Spirit.

These people wanted to build on the great truths uncovered by previous people of vision. God's truth was marching on, turning churches everywhere upside down, and they wanted to march along with it.

You might wonder, "Where is God's remnant today?" Does God have a movement today that stands on the platform of truth erected by the great men and women of faith down through the ages? Is there a church today composed of the doctrinal bricks of faith, laid faithfully by godly men and women of past ages? Is there a movement holding high the torch of truth today?

I believe there is! As a Seventh-day Adventist, I believe the Adventist Church fits the picture of God's remnant people in the book of Revelation. Deeply committed to Christ and His truth, the church leads men and women who love Jesus back to keeping all of God's commandments in preparation for His soon return.

No denomination is perfect. No church can claim that it has no further need of growing in grace and knowledge. Adventists can board up the windows and make a fortress out of their doctrinal positions just like anyone else.

But this is the commitment I'd like to make. By God's grace, I want to hold on to the truth by reaching out for more. I want to be part of a movement, not just a denomination.

Will you join me in that commitment? Will you resolve to keep growing in grace and knowledge, to keep expanding with God's Word, to keep following the principles of Scripture wherever they may lead?

That's the kind of remnant God wants to have today. That's the kind of people who will help bring history to a climax. That's the kind of faith that will triumph over any and every adversity. Let's join together—right now—to take the next step forward, to discover for ourselves God's truth.

If your heart burns with an intense desire to follow God's truth, why not pray this prayer right now!

* * * * *

Father, You can see into our hearts right now; You know what steps we need to take. There are truths we need to understand more deeply, principles we need to apply more consistently. Please don't let us just camp out inside whatever doctrinal fortress we were born in. Help us to be flexible in Your hands. Help us right now to hold on to the truth by reaching out for more. In Jesus' name, I pray. Amen.

Spiritual Babylon Revealed

The book of Revelation describes the church as a pure woman. Christ is her husband; the church is His bride. Christ, the head of the church, gives guidance and direction to His bride. The Bible pictures the true church as a pure woman—one who is faithful to her husband, one who has not committed spiritual adultery. The false church is represented in the Bible by a harlot, or an adulteress, who has left her true lover, Jesus Christ, and united with the world.

In a moving drama, John the Revelator describes one of the most significant moments in human history:

> A great sign appeared in heaven: a woman clothed with the sun, with the moon under her feet, and on her head a garland of twelve stars. Then being with child, she cried out in labor and in pain to give birth (Revelation 12:1, 2).

According to Scripture, this child was to rule all nations with a rod of iron. Ultimately, He was "caught up to God and to His throne" (verse 5). Obviously, this is a description of Jesus.

The Bible says this woman stands on the moon. As the moon reflects the glory of the sun, so the Old Testament church could only reflect the glory of the gospel that blazed forth in Jesus. As the Old Testament dispensation faded away, the New Testament church, clothed with the glory of Christ, arose in splendor. The garland of twelve stars on the woman's head signifies that the church is not guided by human administrators but by divinely inspired apostles. Here is a picture of God's true church, clothed with the righteousness of Christ, having divinely guided, spiritual administrators. What a beautiful symbol of the pure, true church, unadulterated by human traditions, untouched by human doctrine, based on the Word of God. Yet the picture dramatically changes in Revelation, chapter 17. John's vision in this chapter stands in sharp contrast to the one in chapter 12.

> He carried me away in the Spirit into the wilderness. And I saw a woman sitting on a scarlet beast which was full of names of blasphemy, having seven heads and ten horns. The woman was arrayed in purple and scarlet, and adorned with gold and precious stones and pearls, having in her hand a golden cup full of abominations and the filthiness of her fornication. And on her forehead a name was written: MYSTERY, BABYLON THE GREAT, THE MOTHER OF HARLOTS AND OF THE ABOMINATIONS OF THE EARTH (Revelation 17:3-5).

This jeweled woman passes around the wine of her false doctrines, and the world becomes drunk. She is a harlot; she has left her true lover. She is not the true church of Christ, but the false church. She is the mother of many other false churches. Let's study these two women and hear God's call to our hearts.

In the book of Revelation, the Bible describes a great war that took place thousands of years ago in heaven:

> War broke out in heaven: Michael and his angels fought against the dragon; and the dragon and his angels fought, but they did not prevail, nor was a place found for them in heaven any longer. So the great dragon was cast out, that serpent of old, called the Devil and Satan, who deceives the whole world; he was cast to the earth, and his angels were cast out with him (Revelation 12:7-9).

In heaven, Satan attempted to deceive the loyal angels. After he was cast out into the earth, he lied to Adam and Eve in the Garden of Eden. In effect, he said, "Eve, you can eat of that tree, and you won't surely die. All the trees in the garden are the same. It doesn't make any difference whether you eat of that tree or not." Thus, Satan sowed his first lie on earth.

The woman in white

The Bible teaches that there are two great systems of religion. One is centered in Jesus, who is "the way, the truth, and the life" (John 14:6). It is based solidly on the teachings of Scripture. Consequently, in Revelation 12, the true church is pictured as a woman in white. Her doctrines are pure; she is loyal to her true Master. She has not compromised the truth. Truth and error, as water and oil, cannot and do not mix. God is looking for a church that does not mingle truth and error. He is looking for a people who are living in harmony with the truth of His Word. The woman in white of Revelation 12 represents God's true, visible church on earth, His faithful people through the ages who have not compromised Bible doctrine.

The woman in scarlet

As we have seen, in addition to the woman in white, the Bible describes a woman in scarlet with a cup of wine in her hand, representing false doctrine. She is the great apostate mother church, and many churches have drunk of her wine. The Bible says that she rides upon a scarlet-colored beast. In the Bible, a beast represents a political system.

This false church, adorned in scarlet and purple colors, is the mother of harlots. In other words, she has left her true lover, Jesus, by placing human traditions and the decrees of church councils above the Word of God. She is an adulteress in the sense that she has betrayed scriptural teachings. She is the great mother church, and along with her are other churches that also have left the true biblical doctrines.

Notice Revelation 17:5: "On her forehead a name was written: MYSTERY, BABYLON THE GREAT." This apostate mother church of Revelation 17 actually retains principles of Old Testament Babylon. In Old Testament times, literal Babylon was a false religious system. God's true church was the nation of Israel. In New Testament times, the Christian church becomes spiritual Israel. Through the apostle Paul, the Lord says, "If you are Christ's, then you are Abraham's seed, and heirs according to the promise" (Galatians 3:29). The woman in white represents true spiritual Israel, Christ's true followers. Again the Lord says, "He is not a Jew who is one outwardly, . . . but he is a Jew who is one inwardly" (Romans 2:28, 29). Individuals of every nationality who accept Jesus and His doctrines become His true followers. They become His chosen people today, just as Israel was His chosen people in Old Testament times.

In Old Testament days, literal Babylon established a

counterfeit system of worship. In the same way, spiritual Babylon represents counterfeit worship in the book of Revelation. Spiritual Babylon continues the principles of Old Testament literal Babylon in its religious observances.

Characteristics of spiritual Babylon

Who is this woman in scarlet? What are these Old Testament Babylonian principles she duplicates? Revelation 17:2 describes her as committing fornication with the kings of the earth. Fornication is an illicit union. "The inhabitants of the earth were made drunk with the wine of her fornication" (verse 2). Therefore, Revelation's picture of a woman on a scarlet-colored beast represents a union of church and state. The emphasis here is the dominance of the church over the state powers—the woman *riding* the beast. The Bible predicted that this false church, in passing around its wine cup, would lead multitudes to drink of its false doctrines, depicting the acceptance of error in the place of truth.

The Bible shows that there are two basic systems of religion: the true system, outlined in Revelation 12, and the false system, outlined in Revelation 17. It is true that not everyone in the true church will be saved. There are some in it who do not have a heart experience with Jesus. A denominational label does not save any individual. The Bible also says that there are many in the false church who know Jesus and love Him but who do not know all the truth for earth's last hour. God is attempting to lead every man, woman, and child from the false system to the true system.

Notice carefully what is written on the forehead of the woman in scarlet: "MYSTERY, BABYLON THE GREAT" (verse 5). After the Flood, wicked people defied God; they disobeyed His word, established their own religion, and erected the Tower of Babel. It was here that God confused their languages. The city of Babylon was later built on the site of the Tower of Babel. The name *Babylon* sounds like the Hebrew word for confusion, recalling the confusion of languages at Babel.

Commenting on the symbolic woman, Babylon, who rides on the scarlet beast, Robert Jamieson, A. R. Fausset, and David Brown say, in their *Bible Commentary*: " 'State and Church are precious gifts of God. But the State being desecrated . . . becomes *beastlike*; the Church apostatizing becomes the *harlot'* " (593, emphasis supplied).

Babylon—a human system

Let's go back to the Old Testament and look at five identifying features of Babylon there. In Genesis 10:8-10, the Bible describes the origin of the city of Babylon. "Cush begat Nimrod: he began to be a mighty one in the earth. He was a mighty hunter before the Lord. . . . And the beginning of his kingdom was Babel" (verses 8-10). The founder of Babel (later called Babylon) was a rebel against God who led out in establishing a system contrary to God.

In the days of Daniel, Nebuchadnezzar boastfully claimed, "Is not this great Babylon, that I have built for a royal dwelling by my mighty power and for the honor of my majesty?" (Daniel 4:30). As Lucifer before him, Nebuchadnezzar had "I" trouble. Spiritual Babylon is a man-made system of religion with an earthly, human leader substituting his headship for the headship of Christ.

The true church of God directs men and women to Jesus Christ as its only head. The false system directs men and women to human spiritual leaders rather than to Jesus, alone, as our great High Priest. Speaking of

Jesus, the Bible says, "He is the head of the body, the church, who is the beginning, the firstborn from the dead, that in all things he may have the preeminence" (Colossians 1:18).

The Bible says that the true church of God does not have an earthly head, but rather, a heavenly one. Someone has said, "The true church of God is the only organization so big that its body is upon earth, but its head is in heaven." The true church of God points men and women to Jesus, who can forgive their sins and release them from the bondage of sin. Revelation's spiritual Babylon is an earthly system of religion based on human tradition with a human leader. Let's summarize. The first two characteristics of the false religious system of Babylon are: (1) accepting tradition above the truths of God's Word and (2) having a human, earthly head of the church rather than Christ.

Babylon—a system centered in image worship

Let's notice a third characteristic of ancient Babylon: Babylon is the source of idolatry.

It is only as we understand ancient Babylon in the Old Testament that we can understand who spiritual Babylon is and God's call to come out of her. Dr. Alexander Hislop states: "Babylon was the primal source from which all these systems of idolatry flowed" (*The Two Babylons*, 12). In the Old Testament, Babylon was a center of image worship. The great temples of Babylon were filled with images of the Babylonian gods before which pagan worshipers bowed in reverence. God's sanctuary at Jerusalem had no such images. In the New Testament Christian church, individuals were instructed to worship Christ directly. There was to be no worship through images.

The Bible plainly states,

You shall not make for yourself any carved image, or any likeness of anything that is in heaven
above, or that is in the earth beneath, or that is in
the water under the earth. You shall not bow down
to them nor serve them (Exodus 20:4, 5).

The Scripture instruction is plain. If images are introduced into worship, it is highly likely that the image
will be considered sacred and receive the homage due
to God alone. History testifies that this has happened
repeatedly. Images have been reverenced and kissed;
relics have been considered holy; statues are embraced
as gods.

God intended that the true system of religion should
lead men and women to worship Him directly, without
the use of images, allowing His Holy Spirit to impress
their minds. Babylon would lead men and women to follow traditions of men, to put preeminence in an earthly
leader, to incorporate images in its worship.

Babylon—ancestor worship

There is a fourth identifying feature of ancient
Babylon that also applies to spiritual Babylon: the concept of an immortal soul that lives on after death. In
Ezekiel 8:13 the Bible says, "He said to me, 'Turn again,
and you will see greater abominations that they are
doing [that is, greater abominations than worshiping
idols].'" Verse 14 adds, "So He brought me to the door of
the north gate of the Lord's house; and to my dismay,
women were sitting there weeping for Tammuz."

Who was Tammuz, and why were the women weeping?

Tammuz was the Babylonian god of vegetation. The
Babylonians believed that when spring gave way to summer and the summer heat scorched the crops, Tammuz

died. Therefore, they wept and prayed that he might return from the underworld. The concept of the immortal soul does not come from the Bible. It slipped into the Christian church through Babylonian beliefs. Its roots are in Babylon, yet the doctrine was fully developed in Greek philosophy. The following quotations clearly describe the origin of the pagan doctrine of immortality. The first is from Amos Phelps, a Methodist-Congregational minister, who lived from 1805 to 1874:

> This doctrine can be traced through the muddy channels of a corrupted Christianity, a perverted Judaism, a pagan philosophy, a superstitious idolatry, to the great instigator of mischief in the Garden of Eden. The Protestants borrowed it from the Catholics, the Catholics from the Pharisees, the Pharisees from the pagans, and the pagans from the old Serpent, who first preached the doctrine amid the lowly bowels of Paradise to an audience all too willing to hear and heed the new and fascinating theology—"Ye shall not surely die" (Amos Phelps, *Is Man by Nature Immortal?*).

Listen to this statement from Justin Martyr, an early church leader, who died in A.D. 165:

> If you have fallen in with some who are called Christians, but who do not admit this [the truth of the resurrection], and venture to blaspheme the God of Abraham, and the God of Isaac, and the God of Jacob; who say there is no resurrection of the dead, and that their souls, when they die, are taken to heaven; do not imagine that they are Christians (Justin Martyr, "Dialogue With Trypho," chapter LXXX, *Ante Nicene Fathers,* 1:239).

The Bible is very plain about what happens to people when they die:

> The wages of sin is death, but the gift of God is eternal life in Christ Jesus our Lord (Romans 6:23).

> His breath goeth forth, he returneth to his earth; in that very day his thoughts perish (Psalm 146:4, KJV).

> The living know that they will die; but the dead know nothing (Ecclesiastes 9:5).

The King James Version of the Bible uses the word *soul* approximately sixteen hundred times, but it never once uses the expression *immortal soul*. Repeatedly, Scripture affirms that only God has immortality (see 1 Timothy 6:16). It was the Babylonians who held the concept that an immortal soul left the body at death. Therefore, the Babylonians established a system of gods and goddesses, worshiping the spirits of those who supposedly lived on. God's people, the Israelites, had a totally different belief. They taught that when people died, their breath went forth, they returned to the earth, and in that very day their thoughts perished. The Bible is a very reliable source regarding the state of humans in death. Psalm 115:17 says, "The dead do not praise the Lord, nor any who go down into silence." Any voice that purports to break death's silence is out of harmony with the Bible.

Friend, Revelation describes two great systems of religion. The true system, referred to in Revelation 12, is based on the Word of God, with the pure doctrines of His Word leading men and women to trust Jesus alone. It leads them to understand that they are to come to

Christ and worship Him directly, without images. It leads them to understand that when people die, they sleep until the resurrection. It affirms the biblical truth that the soul is not some conscious entity that lives on endlessly in the spirit world after death.

Revelation 17 describes a false religious system it refers to as Babylon the great, the apostate mother church. This church is based, not on the Word of God, but on tradition. It has an earthly head that claims to take the place of Christ. Its colors are scarlet and purple. It utilizes images in its worship service. In the place of gods and goddesses, it incorporates saints in its worship services. It teaches that when people die they do not sleep until the resurrrection, but rather have immortal souls that live on after death. It passes its false wine cup around so that other churches drink the wine of false doctrine of this mother church. They, too, accept the false idea that the soul lives on after death—outside of and independent of the body.

Babylon—the center of sun worship

A fifth characteristic of Babylon, both in the Old Testament and in the New, is mentioned in Ezekiel 8:16. This is, in fact, the key principle defining Babylon:

> He brought me into the inner court of the Lord's house; and there, at the door of the temple of the Lord, between the porch and the altar, were about twenty-five men with their backs toward the temple of the Lord and their faces toward the east, and they were worshiping the sun toward the east.

The prophet Ezekiel saw these men following the Babylonian practice of sun worship. Turning their faces toward the east, they knelt and worshiped the sun god as the sun rose in the eastern sky. Ancient Babylonian calendars, with the sun at the center, reveal the importance the Babylonians placed on sun worship. The Babylonians did not believe that they were fashioned by the hands of a loving Creator. They believed the sun, the largest luminous body in the heavens, was the source of life. In adoration, they bowed to worship it. "In ancient Babylonia the sun was worshipped from immemorial antiquity" (James G. Frazer, *The Worship of Nature*, 1:529).

The Israelites worshiped the Creator on the seventh day of the week, the Bible Sabbath. The Babylonians worshiped an object of creation, the sun, on the first day of the week. God's true church in Revelation 12 keeps all His commandments, including the Sabbath. The false church revives the Babylonian day of the sun and passes around its cup of false doctrines. Many churches, drinking from that cup, worship on the first day of the week, Sunday.

God has a sign: "I also gave them My Sabbaths, to be a sign between them and Me, that they might know that I am the Lord who sanctifies them" (Ezekiel 20:12). All through the Old Testament, on into the New Testament, and until the end of time, God's Sabbath is a sign—an everlasting symbol of allegiance to our Creator.

The pagan Romans also showed special reverence to the sun. As church and state united in the early centuries, sun worship slipped into the church. Arthur P. Stanley says:

> Sunday, is, in a great measure, owing to the union of Pagan and Christian sentiment with which the first day of the week was recommended by Constantine to his subjects Pagan and Christian alike, as the 'venerable' day of the sun *(His-*

tory of the Eastern Church, 184).

Note Stanley's statement well. He says there was a compromise measure, a union of paganism and Christianity, in the early centuries, and thus Sunday slipped into the Christian church. Church and state, the woman and the beast, united. The Babylonian principle of sun worship, that pagan principle passed down from one pagan religion to the next, slipped into the Christian church, not by a commandment from God, but rather by human tradition.

Stanley further states: "[Constantine's] coins bore on the one side the letters of the name of Christ; on the other the figure of the Sun-god, . . . as if he could not bear to relinquish the patronage of the bright luminary" (ibid.). Amazing! On Constantine's coins, Christ's name was written on one side, and the sun god was pictured on the other side. A wedding took place between Christianity and paganism, between the church and the pagan emperor of Rome. Constantine was actually a Christian only in name. As a result, the Christian church was flooded with many practices that do not find their place in Scripture. Bible history bears this out. Dr. Alexander Hislop says,

To conciliate the Pagans to nominal Christianity, Rome, pursuing its usual policy, took measures to get the Christian and Pagan festivals amalgamated, and . . . to get Paganism and Christianity—now far sunk in idolatry—in this as in so many other things, *to shake hands* (*The Two Babylons*, 105, emphasis supplied).

In other words, Rome was attempting to conciliate, to compromise, to bring the crumbling empire together.

What is the origin of Sunday worship? Where does it come from? How did it enter the church?

Dr. Edward T. Hiscox, author of *The Baptist Manual*, stated in a paper before a Baptist convention of ministers on November 13, 1893: "What a pity that it [Sunday] comes branded with the mark of paganism, and christened with the name of the sun god, then adopted and sanctioned by the papal apostasy, and bequeathed as a sacred legacy to Protestantism!"

The door was opened, as Babylonian practices flooded into the church. Catholics say, "Christendom is indebted to the Catholic Church for the institution of Sunday as the Sabbath day. But there is no precedent in Scripture, nor commandment in Scripture, to observe the Sunday as the Sabbath day" (*Our Sunday Visitor*, 4 January 1931).

In the fourth century, in an attempt to convert the pagans and save the empire, church leaders opened that door. The Roman emperor, Constantine, who had, on the surface, become a Christian, walked through that door, and church and state thus united. Babylonian sun worship slipped into the Christian church as a union between paganism and Christianity took place.

F. G. Lentz says, "In keeping Sunday, non-Catholics are simply following the practice of the Catholic Church for 1,800 years, a tradition, and not a Bible ordinance" (*The Question Box*, 99).

You remember, we read in Ezekiel 8:16 about the twenty-five priests of Israel who adopted the practice of sun worship. These priests turned their backs on the true God, rebelled against His law, and disobeyed His direct command to observe the seventh-day Sabbath. Ezekiel described the real issue in this drama between good and evil:

Her priests have violated My law and profaned My holy things; they have not distinguished between the holy and unholy, nor have they made known the difference between the unclean and the clean; and they have hidden their eyes from My Sabbaths, so that I am profaned among them (Ezekiel 22:26).

God said that in ancient Israel the priests hid their eyes from His Sabbaths, and He was profaned among them. In the last days, the Babylonian principle of sun worship will be adopted. Again, people will hide their eyes from the true Sabbath. Men and women will say, "It doesn't really make any difference." Oh, my friend, it *does* make a difference.

James Wharey says:

At the end of the second century, . . . it is obvious to mark the changes already introduced into the Christian church. Christianity began already to wear the garb of heathenism. The seeds of most of those errors that afterwards so entirely overran the church, marred its beauty, and tarnished its glory, were already beginning to take root (*Church History*, Century II, section VII).

Yes, the wedding took place, and the seeds of human tradition grew and developed. Dr. Alexander Hislop adds,

This tendency . . . to meet Paganism half-way was very early developed. . . . Upright men strove to stem the tide, but . . . the apostasy went on, till the Church, with the exception of a small remnant, was submerged under Pagan superstition (*The Two Babylons*, 93).

After Christ died and the apostles passed off the scene, the church drifted from its original teachings. Nevertheless, there were a small remnant who remained loyal to God. Down through the ages, God has always had those who have said, "We will not compromise; we must stand for truth, no matter what the popular masses are doing. We have submitted our lives to Christ. He has said, 'If you love Me, keep My commandments' (John 14:15). We will take the Word of God as our guide. We will stand loyally for Jesus."

At times, that small remnant were oppressed and persecuted. Still, they would not accept the Babylonian principle of tradition above the Scriptures. They would not accept the Babylonian principle of a human, earthly head of the church rather than Christ. They would not accept the Babylonian principle of images. They worshiped Jesus directly. They would not accept the Babylonian principle that there is an immortal soul which lives on, outside the body. They would not accept the Babylonian principle of sun worship. Often they were persecuted and fled from the cities to the valleys, rocks, and mountains.

Friends, an understanding of what the Bible teaches leads us to see that the woman in scarlet pictured in Revelation 17 is the Roman Church. Her daughters are the Protestant churches that have been sipping from her wine cup and accepting her errors. But even in the Roman Church, God has a people. In their commentary, Jamieson, Fausset, and Brown put it this way: "Even in the Romish Church God has a people: but they are in great danger; their only safety is in coming out of her at once" (593).

I've had people say to me, "Pastor, can't I stay in my church and reform it?" God says that you are to come out of Babylon. "In every apostate or world-conforming

Church there are some of God's invisible and true Church, who, if they would be safe, must come out" (ibid.).

Do you believe the Bible, God's Word, is more important than tradition? Have you accepted Christ as your personal Saviour? Do you believe Jesus is really coming again? Have you accepted the truth about the Bible Sabbath and the state of human beings in death? You may be wondering, "Can I believe the truth and remain just where I am?" Friend, in every apostate or world-conforming church, there are members of God's invisible, true church, who, if they would be safe, must come out. God calls you to come out, because Babylon is fallen.

The noted Catholic author, Cardinal Gibbons, says: "Reason and sense demand the acceptance of one or the other of these alternatives: either Protestantism and the keeping holy of Saturday, or Catholicity and the keeping holy of Sunday. *Compromise is impossible*" (*Catholic Mirror*, 23 December 1893, emphasis supplied). I agree with Cardinal Gibbons completely on this point. The Catholic cardinal was right when he said that compromise is impossible! These issues are too clear. They demand a choice. This evidence demands a verdict. God is calling men and women to take a stand.

Listen to the words of Scripture: "He cried mightily with a loud voice, saying, 'Babylon the great is fallen, is fallen'" (Revelation 18:2). The mother church is fallen. Her traditions are fallen. This church, with vestments of scarlet and purple, is fallen. Her system of images is fallen. All systems that teach error regarding the state of people in death and the Sabbath are fallen. They have drifted away from Scripture as the only rule of faith and practice.

"I heard another voice from heaven saying, 'Come out of her, my people, lest you share in her sins, and lest you receive of her plagues' " (verse 4). There is no way to stay in Babylon without sharing in her sins. Babylon is fallen! There is no way that you can change her. Your mission, your business, is to come out.

God is calling honest-hearted men and women out of those churches that have drunk the cup of Babylon. Soon, time is going to run out. Soon, every human being is going to make his or her final choice, fully for Christ or fully for tradition, either on the side of truth or on the side of error, standing with the Scriptures or standing with human beings and human substitutes.

Our only safety is in coming out of every church that is based on tradition, that uses images in its worship, that has sipped the wine cup and is still practicing Sunday worship, that believes in the immortality of the soul. God's appeal is to come out.

Jesus said, "My sheep hear My voice, and I know them, and they follow Me" (John 10:27). He says, "My child, I am appealing to you. I have My sheep, My followers, in every church. I am appealing to people of all denominations to lay aside their preconceived opinions and follow the Bible. I am speaking to hearts everywhere to come out of those churches based on tradition."

Oh, I appeal to you, my friends. I appeal to you in Jesus' name to surrender your will to Him and to determine to do His will. With your Bible in your hand, tell Jesus, "I can do no other; I must come out. I hear Your call to my heart. I see how paganism and Christianity united in those early centuries. I see the issue very clearly now. I see that for more than eighteen hundred years, compromise has taken place. I see that God has been calling His little remnant out, and I have decided to take my stand for You, Lord Jesus. I decide to stand on the Word of God; I decide to stand with Christ. I am willing to come out, even if it means standing alone."

Oh, friend of mine, will you not settle it in your heart right now? Will you not seal it in your mind? Will you not tell Jesus, "Lord, I hear Your call that Babylon the great is fallen. I hear You urging, 'Come out of her, My people' "?

Tenderly, in tones of love, Jesus, by His Spirit, speaks to your heart. With lovingkindness He says, "I love you, My child. I do not want you to be afflicted when the plagues fall. My child, I am appealing to you right now!" Some of Jesus' people are still in Babylon. Do you hear His call right now? Do you hear Him speaking to your heart? I know that right now, you are willing to say, "Jesus, I love You, and I choose to follow You. Because I love You, I desire to be part of Your commandment-keeping people. I hear Your voice gently appealing, 'If you love Me, keep My commandments.' Yes, Lord, I will follow."

* * * * *

Father, You are speaking to our hearts, just now. You are asking us to come out of the confusion of Babylon and her false teachings. You are asking us to take our stand with Your faithful, commandment-keeping people. Give us the courage to step out in faith and choose to follow You, no matter how difficult. Thank You for making Your will plain in our lives. In Jesus' name, I pray. Amen.

Modern-day Movement of Destiny

The *Yearbook of Churches* lists 244 Protestant denominations in the United States. If you add to this the Catholic Church, the Jewish faith, and the growing number of new, non-Christian religions in the country, you begin to wonder how anyone can possibly identify God's true church. More and more, people are beginning to ask, "Does God have a church today? If so, is it possible to discover His true church?" With so many voices calling, "This way; we have the truth," is there any way that the average person can tell whether God does have a church today?

I have been interested in analyzing why people attend the particular church that they do. Often, as I visit with people, the question of the true church arises. Our discussions have revealed interesting reasons for church attendance. Sometimes people say, "Oh, I'm a member of this particular church because my parents were members, and their parents were members before that. For as long as I can tell, my family have always been members of that church. In fact, I was born into this church, and I've never really questioned it."

Is it sufficient reason to be a member of a particular church simply because you happen to have been born into it or because your parents were members of that church? Let's suppose that you are a Buddhist and don't believe that Jesus is the divine Son of God. Suppose I opened the Bible and showed you texts indicating that Jesus is God's divine Son. Would your response be, "My parents were Buddhists who always went to the Buddhist temple? Their parents were Buddhists. I certainly wouldn't consider changing now"—is that what you would say? Simply because a person is born into a certain religion is no guarantee that it is the true religion, is it?

What about the heathen in remote places of earth? We go to such a person and try to explain to him the glorious grace of Jesus. He says, "Wait a minute. My father was a headhunter, and his father before him was a headhunter." Would you tell him, "If it's good enough for your father, it's good enough for you?" Certainly not. There must be a better reason to join a church than the fact that you were brought up in it or that your parents were members.

Some people say to me, "I'm a member of this particular church because I like the people who go there." But you might also like the people whom you work with. Does that mean you believe exactly as they do? You might shop at a certain store because you like the clerk. Does that mean you condone everything she or he does or believes? Wouldn't you say that it's only fuzzy thinking that leads a person to be a member of a certain church simply because he likes the people who go there?

A definition of the church

There are other people who attend their church because it's close to their house. It's easily accessible, particularly in the winter. They don't have to drive far, and they save on gas. I have to ask you again, "Is that sufficient reason to attend that church?" When we look beneath the surface at some of the reasons people give for belonging to a particular church, we have to admit that they are insufficient, indeed. The only reason to attend any church is outlined very clearly in 1 Timothy 3:15. This text gives us one of the best definitions of the church in all of the Bible. It speaks of the house of God, "which is the church of the living God, *the pillar and ground of the truth*" (emphasis supplied).

The church is to be the foundation of truth. The only reason to attend any church is not because our parents attended, not because our family attends, not because it's close to home, not because we've been members of it all our lives, not because we like the people who go there, but rather, *because we believe with all our hearts that this church is faithful to the teachings of the Scriptures.* If the church you are attending is not following the Scriptures, then God would have you seriously consider whether you are attending the right church.

Yet someone asks, "With the many churches we have today, is it really possible to know that God has a true church in these last days?"

Jesus, talking to the scribes and Pharisees of His day, gives this principle: "If anyone wants to do His [God's] will, he shall know concerning the doctrine, whether it is from God or whether I speak on My own authority" (John 7:17). This is the crucial point. If anyone is willing to do the will of God, he will know whether the doctrine is true or not. Are you willing to do God's will? Have you said, "Lord, I'm opening my heart to You. Whatever You want me to do, I'm going to do it. If it means making a change in my life, I'm willing to make that change"?

If you're not willing to make a change in your life when God reveals truth, you'll never be able to understand truth. If you are content where you are, if you are solid in your position, and you say, "I will never make a change," you will never know God's truth as you should. If your mind is locked to future discoveries, it becomes impossible to really know the truth. Before we can ever know what God wants us to do, deep within our hearts there must be a willingness to say, "Lord, if it means making a change to follow Your truth, I'm going to make that change. Lord, if it means rearranging my life, You make the adjustments, because I want to follow You."

But somebody says, "Can you really be certain of the truth?" Let's assume you do have this inner attitude of willingness. Can you really know the truth? In John 8:32, Jesus Himself answers this question. He says, "You shall know the truth, and the truth shall make you free." Jesus says, "If you want to know the truth, if in your heart you desire to know it, if you're willing to make a change in your life as God points out the truth to you, you will know it." Jesus Himself says, "I will reveal the truth to you in My Word."

The church through the ages

One thing is for certain: Down through the ages, God has always had a church. This world has never been left without a witness for God. Somebody says, "The church is invisible. It's made up of faithful believers within every creed and denomination." It is true that there are faithful men and women of God in every church. Certainly, there are Baptist Christians, Methodist Christians, Catholic Christians, and Pentecostal Christians. There are men and women who love Jesus in every congregation. This, we might say, is the invisible church. But in addition to the invisible body of believers, the Bible teaches that there is a visible church. God has always had a visible group who have honored Him by living in harmony with His will. He has been leading honest, faithful men and women who have been part of the invisible church to this visible body of believers.

Genesis 26:5 is a text about Abraham. At that time, the majority of the world had turned against God, so God called Abraham to be the head of a spiritual family, what we might call His church. Describing Abraham in Genesis 26:5, Scripture gives the foundations of God's true movement. It says God chose Abraham as the head of His spiritual family, His church, "because Abraham obeyed My voice and kept My charge, My commandments, My statutes, and My laws." God's true church, beginning in the days of Abraham, was a faithful body of believers who kept the commandments of God.

Down through the ages, God's church has been characterized as being faithful to Him. It is often stated, "There is strength in numbers." Yet, according to the Bible, God's people have often been in the minority. In fact, most of the time, His church has not been known for its great numbers. It has found its strength, not in numbers, but in its faithfulness to God and His truth. This is what God told His people in the Old Testament:

> You are a holy people to the Lord your God; the Lord your God has chosen you to be a people for Himself, a special treasure above all the peoples on the face of the earth. The Lord did not set his love on you nor choose you because you were more in number than any other people, for you were the least of all peoples (Deuteronomy 7:6, 7).

God said that Israel was a special people to Him, and yet they were the least of all people. But they kept His commandments; they were obedient to Him. When we are looking for a church, we don't drive down the street and ask, "Which is the biggest church?" Throughout Bible history, the true church often has been very, very small. It has been characterized not by its numbers, but by its loyalty to God.

When the nation of Israel drifted away from God, the Bible says that God called out from the nation a small group of those who remained faithful to Him. Throughout history, when a larger group drifts away from God's purpose, He calls out a smaller group. God has always had His people. At times, this group has been very small. But these faithful people have been known, because they have kept the commandments of God. Haggai 1:12 applies a name to this called-out group; it calls these faithful ones *the remnant*. "All the remnant of the people, obeyed the voice of the Lord their God." Israel had drifted away from God. They began worshiping idols and adopting other customs of the pagans around them. God drew out of them a small group that He called a "remnant." The word *remnant* means the "remaining ones." This remnant was faithful to God; the Bible says they obeyed His voice.

Down through the ages, God has had a visible church, from the time of Genesis to Abraham; then He chose the nation of Israel. And when Israel departed from God's original plan, He called out a remnant group of people who were prepared to receive Jesus when He came and was born in Bethlehem. These faithful ones became the nucleus of the New Testament church. For a while, this church remained faithful, but as it began to drift, God again called out a remnant. "Even so then, at this present time there is a remnant, according to the election of grace" (Romans 11: 5). Paul says God had His remnant people who remained loyal and true in New Testament times. And He has His remnant who remain faithful today, as well.

Now, let's summarize. In the days of Abraham, God had a group who obeyed His commandments. This group, called out to form a church, became the nation of Israel, God's special people, because they kept His commandments. In time, they drifted away, so God called out another group who, at the close of the Old Testament period, were called the remnant, who were obedient to His commandments. They became the New Testament Christian church. When the Christian church itself began to drift away, God still had His remnant who remained obedient. Consider this! If all through the Bible God has had a remnant who remained obedient to His commandments, isn't it logical He would have a remnant today?

Where is this remnant who are faithful to the commandments of God? Can we discover them? Does the book of Revelation speak of such a remnant? Yes, my friends, it does. A keynote of the book of Revelation is that God will have a remnant in the last days of earth's history. He will have a called-out group, a group who will remain loyal and true to Him at any cost.

Revelation defines the true church

John describes the identifying characteristics of God's last-day remnant in Revelation 12:17. There, he describes a divinely foretold people who demonstrate their loyalty to God through their obedience. John says, "The dragon was enraged with the woman, and he went to make war with the rest [the remnant] of her offspring." So do we see the remnant again? Yes. Have we seen the remnant all the way through the ages? Yes. Has God always had a remnant? Yes.

Notice how John goes on to emphasize that God's last-day remnant "keep the commandments of God and have the testimony of Jesus Christ" (Revelation 12:17). Do you want to find the remnant people of God today? They are those who, in deep love for Jesus and in response to His sacrifice on Calvary, will keep the commandments of God. Three times the book of Revelation describes God's true, last-day church as keeping His commandments. Revelation 14:12 adds, "Here is the patience [the endurance] of the saints; here are those who keep the commandments of God and the faith of Jesus."

God's people, His remnant, in the last days will keep all the commandments, including His Sabbath. According to the Bible itself, any church that does not keep the true Sabbath cannot be the remnant. It may teach good things; it may use the Bible and help people find Jesus. But it is not the remnant of God today. According to Scripture, the remnant of God today "keep the commandments of God."

You ask, "Where is the true church?" Revelation 14:12 echoes back, "Here is the patience [the endurance] of the saints; here are those who keep the commandments of God." So, if you are looking for the true church, look for a church that teaches the necessity of obedience to all the commandments of God, including the Bible Sabbath, from the motive of love for Jesus.

Hasn't God made it simple to discover the identity of His remnant? He has given a clear test. He has made it plain, but men and women try to make it complicated.

Somebody might be thinking, *It doesn't make any difference whether a person keeps the Sabbath or whether a church teaches the importance of obeying the commandments of God today.* But what does your Bible say? "Blessed are those who do His commandments, that they may have the right to the tree of life, and may enter through the gates into the city" (Revelation 22:14). Men and women who have been saved by Jesus Christ, who have been cleansed from their sins by His grace, who are in love with Him, will keep His commandments and thus enter through the gates into that city. Yes, friends, the Bible gives us a test. Is the church you are attending a Sabbath-keeping church? Is it a church that teaches the necessity of obedience?

The Bible says there is another characteristic of God's true church today—His remnant. Revelation 12:17 says that they not only keep the commandments of God, but they "have the testimony of Jesus Christ." The true church of God, His remnant, will keep all His commandments, and it will have something else—the testimony of Jesus. The word *testimony* comes from the word meaning "witness." A witness gives a testimony. God's last-day church will be given a witness from Jesus.

What is this testimony of Jesus?

I fell at his feet to worship him. But he said to me, "See that you do not do that! I am your fellow servant, and of your brethren who have the testimony of Jesus. Worship God! For the testimony of Jesus is the spirit of prophecy" (Revelation 19:10).

"The testimony of Jesus is the spirit of prophecy." Then, God's true movement in the last days is identified by two characteristics: it keeps all the commandments of God, including the Bible Sabbath, and it is guided, or directed, by the gift of prophecy. Where is such a movement today with the twin characteristics of keeping the commandments and having the gift of prophecy?

The rise of a movement of destiny

In the early 1800s, a renewed interest in the second coming of Christ swept like a prairie fire across America. People of a variety of faiths, including many who were once infidels, were looking forward to the coming of Jesus. Pouring over the prophecies of Daniel and Revelation, they eventually settled on the year 1844 as the year of His return. When Jesus did not come, those people were bitterly disappointed. Would the movement of which they had been a part be broken up? Would it be fragmented and disintegrate? They looked higher and saw that Jesus had entered into the Most Holy Place of the sanctuary in heaven to begin His final phase of ministry. They saw that the standard of judgment in that sanctuary was the law of God. They discovered the necessity of keeping the Bible Sabbath. At that time God raised up a young woman, Ellen Harmon, later Ellen White, and gave her the gift of prophecy to guide, to direct, the movement of His church. Out of this prophetic movement emphasizing preparation for Christ's return, the Seventh-day Adventist Church was born.

I am a Seventh-day Adventist, not because I was born a Seventh-day Adventist or because the Seventh-day Adventist church is the largest church in my community. I'm not an Adventist simply because my parents were Seventh-day Adventists. I'm not a Seventh-day Adventist because the Seventh-day Adventist church is the closest to my home; there are many other churches much closer. Friend, I am a Seventh-day Adventist because I believe it is ordained by God to play a special role as His remnant in these last days. God's Word says that in the last days a Sabbath-keeping movement will arise with the inspired guidance of the gift of prophecy.

If I'm going to be faithful to the Scriptures, I have to be part of a Sabbath-keeping movement, because Revelation states:

> Here . . . are those who keep the commandments of God (14:12).

Blessed are those who do His commandments (22:14).

The dragon was enraged with the woman, and he went to make war with the rest of her offspring, who keep the commandments of God (12:17).

Therefore, if I'm going to be part of God's remnant, I have to be part of a commandment-keeping, Sabbath-keeping movement. I have to be part of a movement that is guided by the gift of prophecy. So I'm a Seventh-day Adventist, not because I was born one, but because I cannot do otherwise and still be intellectually honest with myself and with the teachings of Scripture. The Seventh-day Adventist Church is that movement of destiny God has predicted in the book of Revelation. It is that movement which God Himself has pointed out. It has the identifying characteristics Scripture describes.

The message of the true church

Did you know that the Bible actually tells us what God's true church will preach in the last days? What its message will be? We have seen the two identifying features of that church; let's discover the message of the true church. Revelation 14:7 pictures an angel, a messenger, who says with a loud voice, "Fear God and give glory to Him, *for the hour of His judgment has come*" (emphasis supplied). God's last-day message wouldn't say the judgment is off in the future. It would say, "We are living in the judgment hour." The Seventh-day Adventist Church is the only church I know of that teaches we are living in the judgment hour now!

In an age of moral irresponsibility, when men and women feel that they are accountable only to themselves, God has a movement telling them that they are accountable to God. In an age when men and women say, "I am my own god; I can do my own thing," God has a movement pointing out that, as moral creatures, we have accountability in the judgment. He is directing His movement to lead men and women to understand that the clock has struck the hour. No more is it business as usual; no more is it pleasures as usual. We are indeed living in the time when the sands in the hourglass are running out. We are living in the judgment hour.

May I ask you some penetrating questions? Are you part of a movement that's keeping all of God's commandments—including the Bible Sabbath? Are you part of a movement that is proclaiming the message of Revelation to the world? Are you part of a movement that is announcing that the judgment hour is going on in heaven? Friend, God's church proclaims a special message for earth's last hour. This church is not simply a denomination. This is a movement—a movement of destiny that God Himself has raised up, as shown by the prophecies of the book of Revelation.

Notice again, in Revelation 14:7, the message of God's people in the last days of earth's history. The messenger is "saying with a loud voice, 'Fear God and give glory to Him.' " How do we do that? In what way may we give God glory? Let's notice one way:

Do you not know that your body is the temple of the Holy Spirit who is in you, whom you have from God, and you are not your own? For you were bought at a price; therefore glorify God in your body and in your spirit, which are God's (1 Corinthians 6:19, 20).

The book of Revelation says that God's last-day church will say with a loud voice, "Fear God and give glory to

Him." Paul says in Corinthians, "You were bought at a price; therefore glorify God in your body." So the true church, the remnant church, will lead men and women not only to obedience to the Ten Commandments, but also to obedience to the laws of health. God's true church points out the fact that to defile the body is contrary to the will of God. God's true movement in the last days of earth's history speaks to the issues of this age. When men and women are defiling their bodies with alcohol, tobacco, and unclean foods, the true church declares, "Fear God and give glory to Him in what you eat and what you drink." It echoes the words of the apostle Paul in 1 Corinthians 10:31, "Whether you eat or drink, or whatever you do, do all to the glory of God." The message of healthful living is an important part of the true church's message.

My friend, are you part of the church that is calling men and women to give glory to God in what they take into their bodies? This is part of God's last-day message. It's part of the Revelation message. God has a movement, a movement of destiny, a movement that didn't just happen to pop up, that is not simply one of many denominations. It is a movement that He has raised up and of which He has listed the identifying characteristics. It invites men and women to give up alcohol and tobacco, dedicating their bodies as the dwelling place for God's Holy Spirit.

Revelation 14:13 gives another identifying characteristic of God's movement: "I heard a voice from heaven saying to me, 'Write: "Blessed are the dead who die in the Lord from now on." ' 'Yes,' says the Spirit, 'that they may rest from their labors, and their works follow them.' " According to the book of Revelation, God's true church will have the answer to spiritism. While multitudes believe that the soul leaves the body and can communicate with the living, the Bible says that God's last-day church will teach the truth about death. "Blessed are the dead which die in the Lord . . . that they *may rest* from their labors."

Ecclesiastes 9:5, 6 explains further what it means for the dead to rest from their labors:

> The living know that they will die; but the dead know nothing, and they have no more reward, for the memory of them is forgotten. Also their love, their hatred, and their envy have now perished; nevermore will they have a share in anything done under the sun.

Friend, God's true, last-day church will keep all God's commandments, including the Sabbath, and will call men and women back to obedience. It will be guided by the gift of prophecy. It will preach the everlasting gospel that Jesus saves, that sins can be forgiven. It will preach that men and women can be delivered from sin. It will announce that we are living in the judgment hour. It will give people clear direction that their bodies are the temple of God, and it will call for release from alcohol, tobacco, and unclean foods. It will announce the fact that when people die, they sleep in the earth. This is the message of God's movement in the last days of earth's history.

An issue of worship

The Bible also teaches that God's movement in the last days will clearly, fearlessly point out the issues involved in the decision that will face the world regarding worshiping the Creator or receiving the mark of the beast. Revelation 14 tells us that just before Jesus returns there will be two contrasting demands for worship. "Fear God and give glory to Him, for the hour of His judgment has come; *and worship Him who made heaven and earth, the sea and springs of water*" (verse 7, emphasis supplied). Put with that verse 9: "Then a third angel followed them, saying with a loud voice, 'If anyone *worships the beast and his image*, and receives his mark on his forehead or on his hand, he himself shall also drink of the wine of the wrath of God' " (emphasis supplied). The true church will lead men and women to worship the Creator. It will tell them what the mark of the beast is and lead them away from worshiping the beast, who has changed the law of God and claims that the change is a sign of his authority. Yes, God has raised up a movement—men and women from every faith, men and women of every creed, who are being led by His Spirit. They are sensing that God has a movement specifically outlined in the book of Revelation.

There are many sincere Christians who have not yet understood God's special message for today. Just before His soon return, He reaches out to lead them to the truths of the book of Revelation so that they can become part of His movement of destiny—a movement that will sweep the world with vital truths in earth's final hour. His church will restore the truths that have been lost sight of down through the ages. His people hear His voice calling them, speaking to their hearts. They sense that God has a movement in these last days of earth's history.

But someone asks, "If the church that I am attending was good enough for my parents, if it was good enough for my grandparents, it must be good enough for me." Why do we believe that the religion of our grandparents is adequate for us, when we don't feel that way in other areas of our lives? Would you be satisfied with the medical practices that were "good enough" for your grandparents? Think of the advances that have taken place in the field of medicine down through the ages. George Washington, the first president of the United States, died, partially, because the doctors of his day believed that if a person had a fever, he had too much heated blood; it was necessary to bleed him. Therefore, Washington's veins were cut, and he was bled. In that weakened condition, he died. Would you submit to the barbaric medical practices of a century or two ago?

Just as there have been advances in science through the centuries, God's truth has been revealed more and more clearly. In the great period of spiritual darkness during the Middle Ages, truth was mingled with error. But in these last days, God will have a people who will arise to restore the truth about the Bible Sabbath, a people who will be guided by a prophet, a people who will direct men's and women's attention to the fact that the judgment is going on in heaven, a people who will point the whole world to the fact that the body is the temple of God. It will help people quit smoking and overcome alcohol. It will help them to quit eating unclean foods. God will have a people who will teach the truth about death as the answer to spiritism. This movement will warn men and women about the coming mark of the beast.

God's call to you!

Does God expect a person to follow new light, new truth? The psalmist describes the attitude of every true Christian: "Teach me Your way, O Lord; I will walk in Your truth" (Psalm 86:11). When we pray, "Oh, Lord, teach me Your way," God expects us to respond as He reveals truth to us. Have you been praying, longing for truth? Have you been reading this book because you are spiritually hungry? Has your heart been opened? I believe it is God's Spirit who has caused you to read these words. It's the Spirit of God who has wanted you to hear His last-day message—not the message of just another church, but the message of a movement that God has outlined in the book of Revelation.

Time is running out! We are on the verge of the eternal world. Jesus is reaching out around the world, leading men and women to step out and follow, not human doctrines, not the doctrines of some church leaders, but the truth.

Each year in South America, forty to fifty thousand lovely Roman Catholics step out to follow Jesus and accept the Adventist message. Many thousands of the Kasai people in Zaire, Africa, approached the leadership of the Seventh-day Adventist Church a few years ago and said, "As we have considered the religions in our country, we believe that the Adventist Church is the most faithful to the Bible. Would you send missionaries to instruct us?" Thousands have been baptized. In Korea, one thousand were baptized in a single day!

I think of how God is reaching out and touching the lives of some pastors today. A while back, the wife of a Lutheran minister, Pastor C. Raymond Holmes, with a congregation of six hundred members, began to study the Bible. As she studied the book of Revelation, she began to discover God's truth. She finally approached her husband and said, "Honey, I've found new light, new truth." The good, but uninformed, pastor opposed her. His wife said, "Honey, I must move ahead. I must follow my conscience." She finally was baptized as a Seventh-day Adventist. Her husband continued to preach on Sunday. But eventually a crisis developed, and Pastor Holmes left the Lutheran ministry. He decided to go to Andrews University, to the Adventist Theological Seminary. He thought, *I will demonstrate that Adventism is not right.* So he enrolled as a student. He was a very open man, and as he attended classes, the Spirit of God touched his heart. At last he said, "I can do only one thing. The Adventist Church is not just another church; it's a movement. I must become a part of it." Today, Raymond Holmes is a Seventh-day Adventist pastor.

I think of a Catholic priest, the editor of the *Catholic Sentinel,* in a particular section of Africa. He was a very kind man, a very loving and conscientious Christian. He studied his Bible earnestly. As he studied, he came to the conclusion that he had accepted things that were not truth, but tradition. After careful study and prayerful consideration, he stepped out to follow the Lord Jesus Christ and became a Seventh-day Adventist Christian.

I think of my good friend, Sammy Jacobson. Sammy wrote the book *The Quest of a Jew,* in which he tells his story. He longed to have peace of mind. Through the study of the Bible, he found Jesus and His truth and was baptized into the Adventist family.

Yes, my friend, God is reaching out, touching lives, young and old, rich and poor. There is a movement that is going around the world, and God is calling men and women to be a part of it. Men and women of all faiths, men and women of all creeds, are responding to God's call. Men and women whom Jesus is leading in a very special way are taking a step in their lives. Men and women whom Christ is calling hear His voice and follow Him.

Friend, it's no accident that you have been reading this book. Of the many millions in the world today, the Spirit of God has led you to this point in your life because He wants to reveal to you something wonderful. The Spirit wants to reveal the glorious fact that God has a movement in the last days of earth's history. So God is calling you. He personally invites you to respond.

He is calling you, not simply to put the information you have learned into your brain, but for you to say, "Dear Lord, I choose to respond. I choose to step out. I choose to become part of Your movement around the world."

Will you not decide that you are indeed going to take that step in your life? That you are going to become part of God's last-day movement—this movement that is reaching out to the ends of the earth? Will you decide you are going to be part of God's last-day movement that has been raised up in harmony with the prophecies of the book of Revelation? Why not, in your heart, seal it with Jesus? Why not, right now, make this a moment of truth? Make it your moment of decision.

* * * * *

Father, we believe that You have a plan for each life. We believe that You bring truth to our hearts at just the right time so that we may respond and step out in faith to follow You. All through the centuries of sin, You have had a people, a church, who remained faithful to You. You have a remnant in these last days before Jesus comes, and we want to be a part of Your true remnant church. Help us to make our decision to follow You. Thank You. Amen.